THE FIRST CHINOOK

The Adventures of Arthur T. Walden
and His Legendary Sled Dog, Chinook

THE FIRST CHINOOK

The Adventures of Arthur T. Walden
and His Legendary Sled Dog, Chinook

BY DAVID PAGEL

WITH WOOD ENGRAVINGS BY RICK ALLEN

THE KENSPECKLE LETTERPRESS · 2005 · DULUTH · MINNESOTA

ISBN 0-9764676-0-7

Publisher's Address:
Kenspeckle Letterpress
394 Lake Avenue South, Suite 701
Duluth, Minnesota 55802

Distributor's Address:
Adventure Publications
820 Cleveland Street South
Cambridge, Minnesota 55008

For Paul

It all begins
With alpine winds…
They churn the snow,
Each crystal spins,

nd rises up
A blinding haze,
A whiteout gale
That lasts for days.
From Fairbanks to the Beaufort Sea
The ice is raked with blown debris.

'Tis then the mushers go to ground,
Make their camps and hunker down.
In igloos, huts and canvas tents,
All huddle round the glowing vents,

Swapping tales from endless trails,
Of aggressive bears, impressive whales,

Rolling bergs and cracking leads,
Of mighty dogs and daring deeds.

And of these last,
There's one they'll tell
That's soothing balm in a frozen hell.
It's true as north,
And grand as gold,
It warms their souls
In the shrieking cold...

The story of the First Chinook!
The Great Chinook!
A recipe without a cook,
A formula that spells success,
Without an author—nonetheless,
It shows to those half froze and numb,
How out of nowhere,
Hope can come.

A hundred years ago, or so,
In old New Hampshire, deep with snow,
Then and there—
That's when and where—
A dog appeared, as if from air.

'Twas in a mother husky's nest,
A golden pup! Unlike the rest,
Something new,
Not just the hue,
But up and down and through and through
A pooch with most peculiar looks,
Like nothing else upon the books.

man named Walden spied the pup,
He pried him out
And eyed him up:
"You are a very different sort,
Your nose is black, your hair is short,"
Said Walden, to the oddball whelp.
"Most of all, I cannot help
But see that you have yellow fur—
You're no husky, that's for sure!"

or Malamute nor St. Bernard…
But," he pondered, looking hard
At snowshoe paws,

And eager tail
That twitched, that itched, to hit the trail,
"Your heart and legs are brick and mortar,
You're a sled dog, made-to-order!"

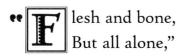 "**F**lesh and bone,
But all alone,"
Mused Walden to the pup unknown.
This puzzle had but one solution:
A doggone leap of evolution!
A breed apart,
A fluke,
A stray,
Orphaned by his DNA!

"Fear not," said Walden, "I will claim you...
But first I think I ought to name you."

"Now let me see, what will it be?
I have it! Something fresh and free
That brings new change, raises hopes,
And wings like spring down frosty slopes.
You're built to move, to howl with joy,
Chinook shall be your name, my boy!"

The First Chinook,
The Great Chinook,
A single dog was all it took...
Poof! From out of empty space:
Woof! A pup with gilded face!
Heaven-sent, like God's own sigh,
Brand new life
Breathed from on high.

hinook soon grew…
And grew…
And grew!
(More horse than dog, was Walden's view)
One hundred pounds from tail to chin,
Huskier than his Husky kin.

nd true to what his master said,
Chinook was born to pull a sled.
The brawny flanks,
Like an armored tank's,
Were made to grade and plow through banks.

Strength of a tractor...
Heart of a spaniel...
All he lacked was an owner's manual!
Chinook was every musher's dream,
And led the pack on Walden's team.

L ike a rifle shot,
As swift as thought,
Their sled could not be slowed or caught,
Oh what a scene!
Oh what a blur!
A meteor of harnessed fur!

Rocketing on paws and rails…
Velocity that glazed the trails
And burst through snowdrifts like a knife,
With Walden gripping for dear life.

They saw such sights:
The Northern Lights!
The feathered frost on corniced heights…
They raced the wind, they chased the sun,
Up even great Mount Washington,
The coldest, wind-swept place on Earth.
'Twas here the grand dog proved his worth,
In arctic weather, snow and rime,
Their sled the first to make the climb!

Yes, everything about Chinook—
His awesome strength,
His handsome look,
His fortitude, like dogged glue,
His disposition, kind and true—
'Twas all so fine, a magic blend…
But was this just the start or end?
Could a dog, sprung from Fates,
Reproduce these ideal traits?
And though the odds were naught to slim,
He fathered puppies, all like him!

T he First Chinook,
The Great Chinook,
A single dog was all it took…
And from that seed,
A brand new breed
Of sled dogs graced with strength and speed,
A race of tawny, yellow hounds,
Each pulled one-hundred-fifty pounds!

And that, for one with such a tally,
Might have been the grand finale.
Fame secured,
His line assured,
Yet Chinook was undeterred.
He set new records without fail,
He conquered every inch of trail,
Raced every valley, gap and town
That laced New Hampshire up and down,
From Dixville Notch to old Portsmouth,
'Til finally Walden took him south…

To a land so stark,
With six months dark,
Where the icecap creaks and huskies bark
At St. Elmo's fire 'round mast and wire
And winds are fierce, as the cold is dire.
Where these elements are loathed and feared,
Where the calendar is just plain weird,
A land without a spring or autumn
That caps the Earth upon its bottom—
Antarctica! The great white place,
On maps and globes, just empty space…
This continent, so long ignored,
Now was ripe to be explored.

’T was Admiral Byrd who ran the show,
Whilst Walden ran his dogs through snow
and sleet to keep the troops supplied—
Chinook, as always, by his side.
Now old in years, yet young at heart
The tireless dog still played a part.
When the others lagged or stalled
’Twas then the famous name was called:

The Great Chinook!
The First Chinook!
A single dog was all it took…
To take command, to gather steam,
To muster strength and move the team.

The men could only watch with awe
This golden wind of fur and paw:
Swirling snow,
Dog bent low,
Sled like lead upon the floe,
But tethered to a gath'ring storm,
A hurricane in canine form!
He roused and spurred the younger mutts
To finally drag it from the ruts.

But life is also like a breeze,
A tiny puff first stirring trees,
It grows until great limbs are bent,
At last it slows, and then is spent.
A dozen years to the day
Chinook was born,
He went away.

And though they searched the tents and shacks,
They found no bones, they found no tracks.
The sled dogs moaned, and Walden wept
That while the darkened camp had slept
The gallant, faithful, much-loved dog
Had vanished into polar fog.

ince that gray and sullen dawn
Chinooks have come,
Chinooks have gone.
But every dog that bears the name

Still carries in its heart and frame
The mystery
Of pedigree
And how the breed first came to be:

The legend of the First Chinook,
The Great Chinook,
The dog that nature gave and took.
Who like a wind that rose and churned,
Appeared from nowhere…

And there returned.

ABOUT THIS STORY

AS A YOUNG MAN, Arthur T. Walden left his native
New England to join in the Alaska Gold Rush of the
1890s. There he became a "dog puncher," driving dog
teams and freighting loads through the brutal cold and
wild beauty of Alaska and the Yukon.

After returning to Wonalancet, New Hampshire, and
a settled life, Walden soon began to miss the excitement
of the far northern trails and began to gather, breed, and
train his own dog sled teams, eventually founding the
New England Dog Sled Club in 1924 (still in existence
today). In 1917 Chinook was born, son of one of Admiral
Peary's Greenland sled dogs and a mixed-breed St.
Bernard. The odd golden-colored puppy, resembling
neither of his parents, soon grew to more than a hundred
pounds with heart and intelligence to match, and
established himself as a natural lead dog and Walden's
constant companion. Chinook proved to be what is
termed a *sport*: a genetic anomaly distinct from its
parents and able to pass its genes on with little variation

to succeeding generations. Walden had a new breed of sled dog, which was simply called Walden's Dog.

Walden and Chinook became celebrities throughout New England and the U.S. during the 1920s as the popularity of sled dog racing began to spread, helped by feats like their first ascent by dog team of Mt. Washington—called the coldest, windiest place on earth.

In 1928 Walden joined Admiral Richard Byrd's expedition to Antarctica as Chief of the Dog Department, and—at 56—the oldest volunteer. Among the almost 100 dogs that went south with Byrd, Walden took Chinook and 18 of his sons.

Now nearly 12 years old, Chinook ran freely beside Walden's sled until a team or a particularly heavy load needed something extra to get it moving, and then he would be hooked into the lead to inspire the other dogs. In his account of the expedition, Admiral Byrd later wrote that, "one sensed that each knew and understood the other perfectly, and it was Walden's rare boast that he never had to give Chinook an order, the dog knew exactly what had to be done."

Before the long Antarctic night began, Chinook

wandered away from camp on January 17, 1929, his twelfth birthday, and was never found. When news of his disappearance from Byrd's Little America was radioed to the U.S., it made headline news around the country and inspired a minor flood of eulogies, stories, and poems from around the world.

When Arthur Walden returned home, he learned that the state wanted to name the road through Wonalancet "The Walden Highway" in his honor. Walden insisted that the road be called "The Chinook Trail" instead, and road signs along Route 113A from Wonalancet to Tamworth, New Hampshire, still carry Chinook's image.

A FEW WORDS ABOUT WOOD ENGRAVING AND THE ARTIST

THE ILLUSTRATIONS for *The First Chinook* are wood engravings, a craft that flourished in the 19th century before the development of photographic reproduction.

Using end-grain blocks of wood (and more recently, composite materials), the artist uses engraving tools with satisfying names like bullsticker, spitsticker, and scorper to cut lines and shapes into the surface. The end-grain of the wood provides a smooth, hard surface that is easily engraved, but is tough enough to allow many impressions to be made without beginning to crumble. Although engravings can be exquisitely detailed, they are often done at a very small scale.

Once the cutting of the image is finished, the block is inked by a roller. A piece of paper is then placed on the block and pressure is applied (either by hand-rubbing or on a press) to take an impression. The ink on the surface of the block will print black while the incised lines made by the engraving tools are left white.

Rick Allen is an artist, printer and printmaker living in Duluth, Minnesota, with his wife and son. His engravings and block-print illustrations have appeared in books, publications and galleries for nearly 20 years.

A FEW WORDS ABOUT THE AUTHOR

AS A LIFELONG mountaineer, Dave Pagel has waited out many a wintry, alpine storm, dreaming of deliverance in the form of the warm, mountain winds known as Chinooks. Also while tent-bound, he regularly found refuge in the ribald adventure verses of Robert W. Service and the Scotsman Tom Patey. Dave credits these experiences and influences as vital inspiration while penning *The First Chinook*.

Dave's previously published work has appeared in *Ascent*, *Rock and Ice*, and *Climbing* magazines—the last where he served as a Senior Contributing Editor.

Dave lives in Duluth, Minnesota (a region that is something of a sled-dog Mecca in its own right) with his wife.